Name_____

©1994 Instructional Fair, Inc.   IF5070 Contemporary Cursive

Name _____

IF5070 Contemporary Cursive

A a

a a

A a A a

Antarctica

astronaut

Amazing aerial acrobats

always accept applause.

B B

b b

B b B b

Barbados

billboard

Busy, bronze bees buzz

beautiful buttercups.

C C

c c

C c C c

California

coconut

Clever circus clowns

create crazy cartoons.

$\mathcal{D}$ $\mathcal{D}$

d d

$\mathcal{D}$ d $\mathcal{D}$ d

Delaware

dachshund

Dieting dinosaurs

don't devour desserts.

Name _____

E E

e e

E e E e

Europe

evergreen

Educated elephants

exercise energetically.

$\mathcal{F}$

f

$\mathcal{F}f$

Florida

firefly

Fantastic fudge fills

four, fat, friendly frogs.

$\mathscr{G}$

g

$\mathscr{G}g$

Gettysburg

gingham

Grouchy gorilla grabs

giggling girls' gum.

HOLLYWOOD

H H

h h

Hh Hh

Honolulu

highchair

Hip, Hollywood hogs

hum harmoniously.

$\mathcal{I}$

i

$\mathcal{I}i$

Illinois

identification

Indestructible insects

invade irate Indians.

J J

j j

J j

Jamaica

journal

Jubilant, jumping

jaguars juggle junk.

K K

k k

K k K k

Kentucky

knuckle

Kindergarten kids keep

kooky knickknacks.

L L

l l

L l L l

Louisville

little

Large, lazy lizards
lick lemon lollipops.

M M

m m

M m M m

Mayflower

memorize

Mischievous mosquitos

make mice mad.

$\mathcal{N}\,\mathcal{N}$

$n\,n$

$\mathcal{N}\,n\quad\mathcal{N}\,n$

Netherlands

nanny

Neptune's nephew needs

nourishment nightly.

O O

o o

O o O o

Ontario

octagon

Orating owls offer odd

opinions on opera.

P P

p p

P p P p

Philippines

pepper

Polite, pink pigs pour

peach punch properly.

Name _____

2Q

q q

2 q 2 q

Quebec

question

Quiet quail quartet

quells queen's qualms.

R R

r r

Rr Rr

Rome

raspberry

Rusty robots require

repeated repairs.

Name _____

$\mathcal{S}$

s

$\mathcal{S}s$

Switzerland

season

See slippery, snoring

snails sleep soundly.

T T

t t

Tt Tt

Tibet

trumpet

The top turtle took

two tennis trophies.

Uu

Uu

UuUu

Utah

unusual

Unforgettable unicorns

unfurl umbrellas.

Name _____

V V

v v

V v V v

Vancouver

velvet

Vacationing visitors

view volatile volcano.

W W

w w

Ww Ww

Washington

watchword

White whales wonder

where walruses winter.

Name _____

TO X-RAY

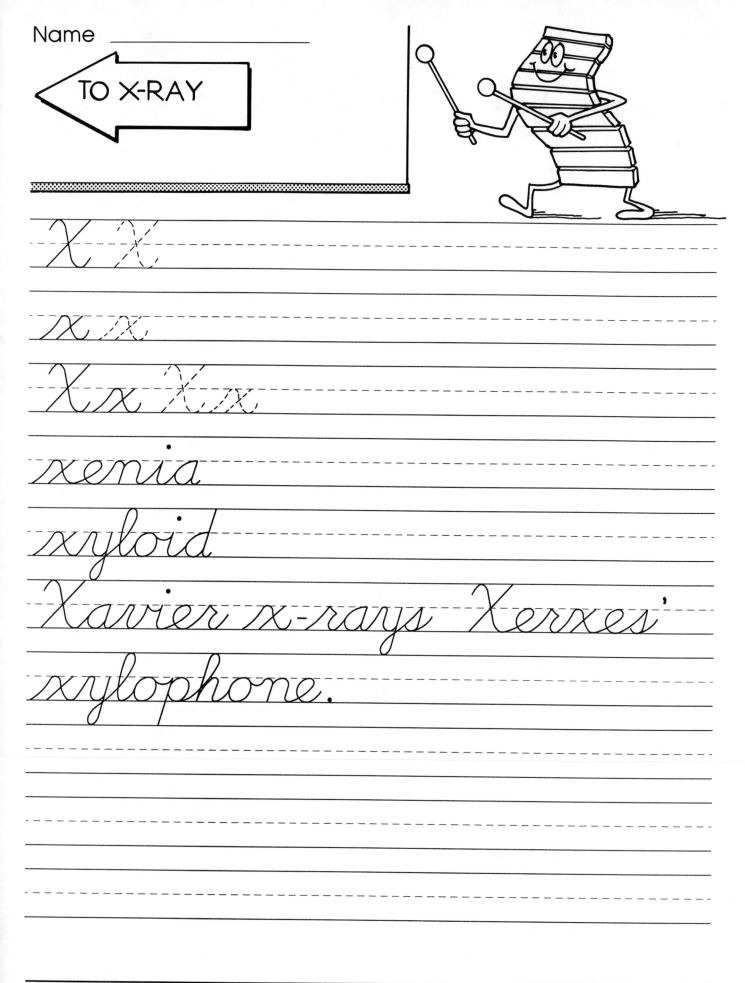

X X

x x

Xx Xx

xenia

xyloid

Xavier x-rays Xerxes'

xylophone.

Yy

Yy

Yy Yy

Yellowstone

yo-yo

Young, Yankee yeoman

yells, "Yonder!"

Z z

Z z

Z z   Z z

Zurich

zipper

Zimbabwe's zany zebras

zigzag zealously.

Name _____

Numerals and Number Words

1234567890

Trace and write.

1 one

2 two

3 three

4 four

5 five

6 six

7 seven

8 eight

9 nine

10 ten

Name _____

Days of the Week

Trace.

Friday   Wednesday

Sunday   Thursday

Tuesday   Monday

Saturday

Write the days in order two times.

Name _____

Trace and write.

Months of the Year

January

February

March

April

May

June

July

August

September

October

November

December

Name _____

About Me

Write your . . .

Name.

- -

Street number and name.

- -

City, state and zip code.

- -

Area code and telephone number.

- -

School.

- -

Three favorite school subjects.

- -

Three favorite sports.

- -

Favorite TV program.

- -

Three favorite foods.

- -

Favorite book.

- -

Name _____

Sentences

The school play is today.
Copy.

Did you buy a ticket?
Copy.

Meet me at seven o'clock.
Copy.

The curtain is rising!
Copy.

Challenge

Write a word with...

one syllable

two syllables

three syllables

four syllables

three letters

four letters

five letters

six letters

two e's

two o's

ing

er

The Liberty Bell

The Liberty Bell is a true symbol of American independence. The famous bell was rung in 1776 to celebrate the signing of the Declaration of Independence. Cracked in 1835, today the bell hangs in the Liberty Bell Pavilion in Philadelphia.

Copy.

The Pledge of Allegiance

The Pledge of Allegiance is a
solemn oath of loyalty to the
United States. The original
pledge was first recited by
school children in 1892.
In 1954, the words "under God"
were added to the pledge, the
salute to the American flag.

Copy.

Name _____

The Washington Monument

The Washington Monument was built in honor of George Washington. It stands by the Potomac River in Washington, D.C. Covered with white marble, it rises 556 feet in the air.

Visitors to the monument must ride an elevator to get to the top.

Copy.

Capitol Hill

Capitol Hill is perhaps the best
known area in Washington, D.C.
Several important government
buildings are on Capitol Hill,
which rises 88 feet in the center
of the city. Some buildings are:
U.S. Capitol, Library of Congress
and Supreme Court Building.

Copy.

The Pony Express

The Pony Express was an amazing mail delivery service that carried mail across the 1,966 miles between Missouri and California.

Established in 1860, the Pony Express consisted of 400 fast horses, 80 riders and 190 stations.

Copy.

Name _____

Camp David

Camp David is the official retreat for the President of the United States. It is built on the heavily-wooded Catoctin Mountain in Maryland.

Camp David has been a home away from the White House since 1942.

Copy.

IF5070 Contemporary Cursive

We the People

The Constitution

The Constitution is the set of
laws which governs our country.
The Constitution was signed on
September 17, 1787, at Independence
Hall in Philadelphia.
It explains the aims of our
government and lists the rights
of each American citizen.

Copy.

Old Ironsides

The "Constitution" better known
as "Old Ironsides," is the oldest
warship afloat in the world.
"Old Ironsides" was launched
in 1797 and fought in the War of
1812. Now docked at the navy yard
in Boston, the ship underwent
reconstruction in the 1800's.

Copy.

Name _____

The Library of Congress
 The Library of Congress, located
in Washington, D.C., is one of the
largest libraries in the world.
It contains over 77 million items,
including 18 million books and
pamphlets.
 Established in 1800, it includes
3 buildings with 71 acres of space.

Copy.

IF5070 Contemporary Cursive

Name _____

The American Eagle

The American Eagle is the
official national bird of the
United States. It was selected
by Congress in 1782.

The American Eagle is found
in all parts of North America.
It has white head, neck and tail
feathers and brown body feathers.

Copy.

The Declaration
of Independence

The Declaration of Independence, signed on July 4, 1776, was a formal announcement that declared our country free from Great Britain's rule. Written by Thomas Jefferson, it stated that the 13 colonies were becoming a new nation, the United States of America.

Copy.

Name _____

The Jefferson
Memorial

The Jefferson Memorial is
dedicated to the memory of
America's third President.
The memorial was dedicated on
April 13, 1943, on the 200th
anniversary of Jefferson's birth.
The white marble building
holds a 19-foot statue of Jefferson.

Copy.

The Smithsonian Institution

The Smithsonian Institution
is a collection of museums, art
galleries, laboratories, a zoo and
educational programs for the
people. Founded in 1846, the
museums display everything
from diamonds to reconstructed
dinosaurs.

Copy.